Maps *and* Transcripts

of the Ordinary World

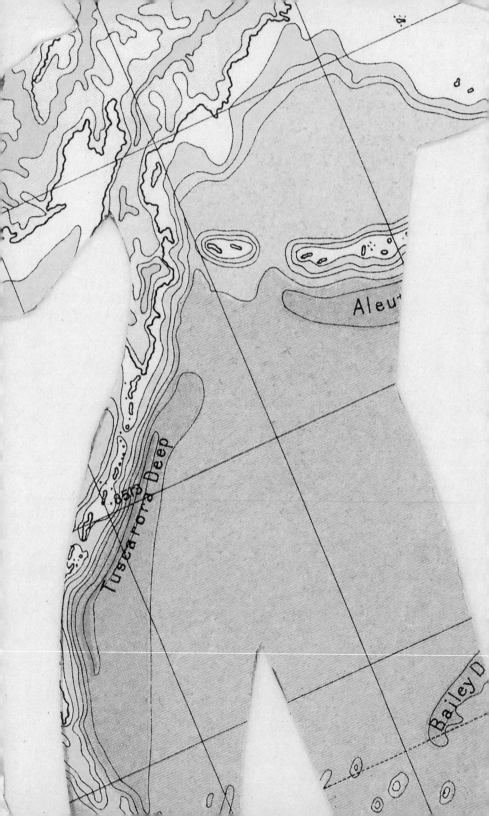

Maps *and* Transcripts
of the Ordinary World

Poems

Kathryn Cowles

MILKWEED EDITIONS

Published 2020 by Milkweed Editions
Printed in the United States of America
Cover design by Mary Austin Speaker
Cover art by Kathryn Cowles
20 21 22 23 24   5 4 3 2 1
First Edition

Milkweed Editions, an independent nonprofit publisher, gratefully acknowledges sustaining support from the Alan B. Slifka Foundation and its president, Riva Ariella Ritvo-Slifka; the Ballard Spahr Foundation; *Copper Nickel*; the Jerome Foundation; the McKnight Foundation; the National Endowment for the Arts; the National Poetry Series; the Target Foundation; and other generous contributions from foundations, corporations, and individuals. Also, this activity is made possible by the voters of Minnesota through a Minnesota State Arts Board Operating Support grant, thanks to a legislative appropriation from the arts and cultural heritage fund. For a full listing of Milkweed Editions supporters, please visit milkweed.org.

Library of Congress Cataloging-in-Publication Data

Names: Cowles, Kathryn, author.
Title: Maps and transcripts of the ordinary world : poems / Kathryn Cowles.

Description: Minneapolis : Milkweed Editions, 2020. | Summary: "Maps and Transcripts of the Ordinary World is a collection of poems about memory, place, and distance between reality and its transcriptions"-- Provided by publisher.
Identifiers: LCCN 2019041953 (print) | LCCN 2019041954 (ebook) | ISBN 9781571315021 (trade paperback) | ISBN 9781571319791 (ebook)
Subjects: LCGFT: Poetry.
Classification: LCC PS3603.O8894 M37 2020 (print) | LCC PS3603.O8894 (ebook) | DDC 811/.6--dc23
LC record available at https://lccn.loc.gov/2019041953
LC ebook record available at https://lccn.loc.gov/2019041954

Milkweed Editions is committed to ecological stewardship. We strive to align our book production practices with this principle, and to reduce the impact of our operations in the environment. We are a member of the Green Press Initiative, a nonprofit coalition of publishers, manufacturers, and authors working to protect the world's endangered forests and conserve natural resources. *Maps and Transcripts of the Ordinary World* was printed on acid-free 100% postconsumer-waste paper by Sheridan Books, Inc.

[For Sue]

CONTENTS

The waters change all the while and stay the same only on the map.

—JOHN BERGER, *To the Wedding*

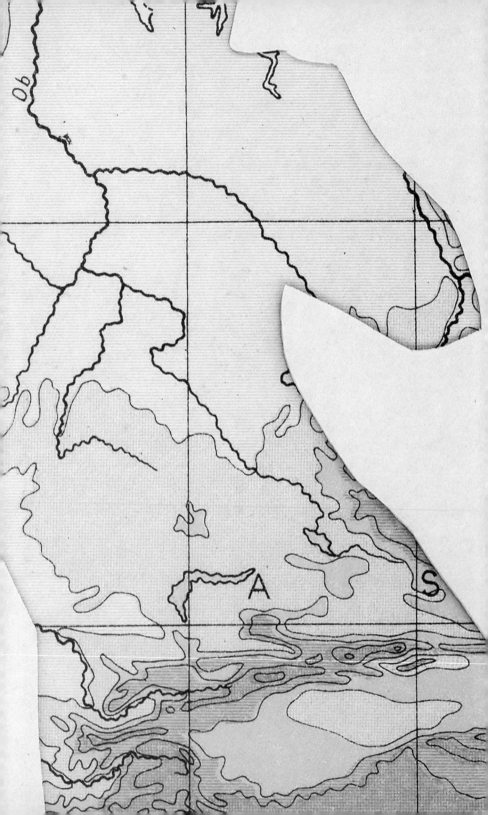

Maps *and* Transcripts *of the* Ordinary World

ORIGIN STORY

I stepped out of the blue paper
of map water
onto an island in Greece
corrugated ground
world was all around me little blue skirt
and I wanted it down
in paper
sun rose and I wrote
sun rose
and then I wrote that I wrote it,
scratch
never in my life
wrapped in paper
have I ever so much
wanted it down

Island

Map

[second bird:] ---------
[to its mother]
[mother gives it some food]

[chews, no swallows, whole]
[1 and 2 sit] [patiently] [wait]
[mother hands it to the black bird
w/ the orange on its face]
[you've got to hand it to her]

HYMN

with 8 birds on a wire

or rather on 3 wires...

    4 birds on 3 wires, one bird on one...

      5 of 'em now on 2;

      on 3; 7 on 4

—EZRA POUND, *THE PISAN CANTOS*

1

all is well, I sang, little
learning how to do the harmony parts,
Saturday church choir, *all is well*

the blue sparrow babies have hatched
and we have kept the cats
away thus far

and one day everyone decides
to bale their hay
every single field down
all at once everyone

all at once
my friend is sick
sick and far away and I hear
will die and I
can't get my head
to think it through
all is well, I sang, *all is well*
tho hard to you

2

so I wrote another friend
a goat on a spit for you, Brenda
we took a photo, I said, transcribed,
put it down, list, list,
sent a postcard
is it getting hot in here

3

I am cycling in the mountains
here is what I see
my arms stretched out in my shadow
three horses facing away

the cows have got out, one white
excuse me while I take this hill

4

don't you call coward on me
I put the knife through the fish's skull
once caught, all alone,
into its hot, hot brain, again, again
to be sure it's just

here lies / the Idaho kid
the only time / he ever did
he transcribed bird bird bird bird in Pisa
counted them for comfort
because everyone needs a latch
comfort, comfort
knife caught hold
in a cliff
and if I die, I sang, *and if I die*

5

the spit is picking up, Brenda
I have a bug in my eye
I can ride a hill down w/ no breaks now
my one eye is streaming from the bug
the spit is turning fast, Brenda
a knife to the brain is quicker
than a whack, whack, more humane
I cannot get it in my head
I see a blue bird, a bale,
a white cow
every single field down
happy day, I sang, *all is well*
every single thing down, picking up

A COMPLETELY DIFFERENT ALPHABET

Transcript. A printed version of a recorded version of a sound. A written version of an audio version of a person talking. A mountain taken down. A printed version of a mountain, printing pressed. A copy. A copy of a copy. The letters pressed into paper resemble the tree's branches. From the Chinese character. A tree. From which issues a bird sound. A printed version of the bird sound, representing the sound a mama bird makes as it feeds its baby birds. A black bird with orange parts. A chicken and an egg. Transliteration. Using the closest corresponding letters or sounds of a completely different alphabet. Shorthand into full sentences. A new arrangement with an entirely other instrument. Transcribed for cello. For piano. For a choir. A bird sound rendered in hyphenated lettering. A mountain. A mountain.

MAP

Two-dimensional circles stand
for three-dimensional hills,
so Profitis Elias (one so called
on every Greek island, the highest point
on which to build a church)
I can tell in advance to be, well,
very tall, but the hewn
marble stairs on the donkey path
are a complete surprise,
    also the donkeys themselves
and their riders with *Yassas, Yassas,*
(one hello for each of us)
    also the view looking down from the top.
I take seven photographs turning
in a circle, a panorama,
but how will I place them hanging
on a wall back home? Something already slipping.

And a world-sized map takes a beating
when it's all spread out,
covers ground but does not match.
And my rugged circles are conceptual, darling.
All they do
is point fingers at loosened hills.

POSTCARD

Dear Brenda, We saw
a lamb on a spit
and took pictures
of it for you,
its bared teeth
and arms tied
and a battery-powered turner,
saw it turn
oh and loved its half-bakedness
for you O Brenda.

And our kitty Artemis
sits on one particular rock
on our rock staircase today,
sits for no reason
and is lovely
and teeming with bugs
though Geoff bathed her in the sink
entirely against her will
though we picked off
two ticks stuck
in her hard
and ugly.

And a ship pulls into the harbor,
pulls in its sails,
wraps them like arms around themselves O
if you could see it.

Map

the way to the ladder

this
a
window

this is a world the size of a world

TRANSCRIPT OF BIRDS

The two birds on the left
sit and the third bird says
[third bird:] ---------

[shakes its wings]

[second bird flies off, back again, off]

[--------- is the bird sound]
[second bird:] [makes the bird sound]
[second bird opens its mouth, shakes
its wings:] ---------
[bug falls on page]
[dead bug]
[from above]
[tree]

THE MAP KEEPS THINGS PUT

1

Every morning we open the curtains.
Every evening we sit on the porch.
We have a topographical map
that names the highest peak
we see out the window.
Two mountain ranges tell us where we are:
We are between two ranges.
Mapped but minus paper.

2

The sea is such today that I can see
on its surface almost the map's white
dot dot dot, the border conceptual.
The map keeps things put.

The islands float above it.
I can see four islands from my perch.
I can be on just one.

3

Enter through the magnetic gate.
Requires pushing.
Path lined with stones
upside-down trees
called umbrella pines
on the left.
There is a door here there is
always a door.

THIS DONKEY PATH

The map is a two-dimensional representation of a three-dimensional swath of land. As I have said. A diagrammatic rendering. For use with a compass. For use with stars. A printed version of the live line between the island and the sea. The island is an island in Greece. The live line is a concept taken down on the page. The line on the page resembles the line between island and sea. Corresponding parts. A record. A miniature. A paper representation of the mountain. A plan. When taken, this donkey path is likely to lead to such and such a village. The village is a pin point. With an invisible edge. Follow the arrow. Follow the red line.

Tide

the shadow maps the shape
of the fortress side
onto the water the water

holds the fortress side
on its shoulder
wraps up in it

LESSON

1

Akis throws water
balloons at the kittens
from the roof.
This is very funny.
Akis is a young boy.
The kittens are young
and have not learned
their lesson.

2

Akis's father shows him
the insides of a motorbike.
This part causes this belt to go,
this belt causes this wheel to turn,
this fan, this timer, this button.
A word that means arrow, means order.
This, that then, then this.

LIST

Table salt.
Chickpea soup
served Sundays.
Rhododendron-
like oleander
comes in pink,
comes in
white.

Green-blue water
peaks with foam
shifting, shifting.

Someone tied a goat
with roped feet
to a bush on the rock.
So it is dead.
We can see
through its body
and smell the inside
of its head.

1. salt
2. goat
3. white
4. cat
5. brine
6. red clay bowl

RECIPE

Goat cheese does not taste like goat smell
does not taste like goat
In short we ate a kid
that had a name but was destined
for slaughter its name was I think Bob
maybe not I made
a goat cheese ball for the occasion

-2 cloves garlic, hand-cut—use a paring knife
  what you want are tiny squares
-handful kalamata olives—a big handful, pitted,
  squares again
-an amount of goat cheese
Use a big bowl mix it w/ your bare hands
shape into a ball
The garlic is strong
give it some bread baked w/ olive oil
to hold onto we all need something

THREE HOURS AT THE BLUE TABLE ON THE TERRACE
IN THE SHADE OF THE ROCK WALL

Geoff in the olive tree and
Akis the upstairs boy, a cat called Baseball,
I see cow and whitewashed garage
lines of terrace holding in olives, figs.
A city with a single wall turns
all houses into neighbors, each to each, touching,
bus goes by
quick write bus chair table boy boat sun down,
down, blue slip of sea.

*

Little girl in the red shirt
sings in the whitewashed garage that catches
even the mean black birds in singing.
La-la-la-la-la-la-la-la-la-la-la
la as in hat
her dad puts her in the back of the
truck still singing.

*

A tree making pomegranates
and one making figs
some citrus
these are tomatoes, those
big purple poofs of onion.

RECIPE

A set of instructions. A list. When taken together, and in this order, and in this way, these things are likely to lead to such and such desired outcome. A loaf of bread. A meat pie. As distinguished from recipient or reciprocity. You give the loaf away to——. You give the loaf and get a meat pie in return. You give the loaf and get a good feeling about. Praise be. A copy of a recipe. Transcribed on a new 3 by 5. For use. Grandma Elizabeth's chickpeas. Traced back to Grandma Lotta's chickpeas. Back to an island in Greece. Sifnos revithada. Stoneware pea pots all dropped to the baker's of a Sunday morning before church. Grandma Appolonia's chickpeas. Pick the pot up after. Some substitutions must be made. ------ for disaster. A copy of a copy. A poor transcription. In shorthand. A completely different alphabet. The original unclear to begin with.

SEA CHANGE

As birds fall
   from great heights right
   outside our window, drop down
   but fly back up easy
   just before hitting the ground,
say mint in a jar

purple picked daisies
   that still close at night
   still love the sun with their wilt.

Say there's a man out the window or
a cat scratching the door
like a strange man
and no telephone,
no way to call out

or fish guts spilled straight
into the Aegean
farther up the beach
or that our skin can burn
can glare sunward so and scratch.

True, paper-eating bugs
have got in the paper paintings
mold in our pillows, rough sheeting
and that we've got to leave
on the ferry on Tuesday,
out with the tide,

but don't say it say instead
love, I love you you sleepyhead get up
get up get up
the sun is.

THE DAY BEFORE THE DAY BEFORE WE HAVE TO LEAVE

From high above, I take three photographs of the same view of the terraces leading to Chrysopigi: whitewashed church on the peninsula-turned-island, its once-neck cracked by God away from the mainland to save monks under attack. Also it is beautiful, this our everyday view from breakfast, and also it is completely ordinary.

I want to commit it to memory. I want to commit it to memory. The photographs slip in place of memory, metaphors for the actual landscape. Transubstantiation. Out of my hands. I sit and watch.

Unmoor

line to port, arrow out
tenuous and white   night sets in

a world is possible but only one
piece at a time

Plain

I AM ON A PLANE

Have I been
on a plane
the greater part
of the day?
I believe I have.
I fall asleep.
I wake up still
on a plane.
I see the sun out
the window I shut
the window shade I go
to sleep. I wake up.
Still on a plane.
I see the moon halved
in the sky in the late
afternoon the same day.
I spend time off the plane
buying food and killing time
till the next plane leaves
and leave it must
and I on it still
I go to sleep.

*

I am asleep on the plane
next to the coffee machines
and I wake up smelling
burnt coffee on hot plates.
I am still on the plane.

The lady dispensing
the coffee is
halfway down the plane
and I am at the end.
Sometimes they start
at the end
but this is not
one of those times.
I go to sleep.

*

I wake up maybe
five minutes later
maybe an hour
maybe we are almost there and
the lady with the coffee
is two rows off,
has she passed me by
once already, asleep,
and come for a second round or
have I been sleeping
for just five minutes.
I don't know.
I open the shade halfway.
Tops of clouds.

*

I wake up and my throat is parched
it feels as though the adjustable air hole
has been blowing directly on
my throat

the lady offers me
pretzels peanuts or cookies
I choose peanuts
she gives me two packages
12 g each, calories from fat 60
well and good
but I am so thirsty.

*

I'm on a plane and
the woman next to me
has a project.
She is tearing the pages
of a magazine
into smaller pieces,
maybe to mark pages
in a book, maybe
for some other reason
but I am trying to sleep
and I am trying to sleep.
The lady puts the torn paper
in her purse
for later use.

*

I try objectifying
the flight attendants.
This is not as fun
as one might think.
And a guy gets up into
the middle of the aisle

and begins his mild
calisthenics
bend, stretch, arms up,
bend, toe touch,
arms up,
rolls his head.

*

The overhead bins
of some sizes of planes
are too small for roller
carry-ons so nothing fits
and this is one of those
sizes of planes,
I am row 37
and my bag is row 28,
had to move all
the plastic-wrapped
blankets to fit it,
over there, I keep thinking,
remember to remember
you are missing parts.

*

Am I getting anywhere?
I must be
if slowly, if bit by bit,
an act of faith
hurtling through the sky
500 miles an hour or more
I put myself in someone else's

hands, nod off, even,
and when I wake
the solid surface of clouds below
looks like a landing pad
in this light.

Paper with tape

sky a wash

a bowl of water

something to hold

the house put

FARM PLOT

Even looking up, it is flat.
Sky stretched tight just
above the trees, great white lid
flat screen projected with
the movie of a sky (no plot)
great white parallel lines, sky, snowy ground,
a whole house gone blank as if caught between mirrors, smaller and smaller.

Sky pieced with light clouds brown white
washed blue new floodwater
and I can tell I am in Ohio just by the sky and
the parallel horizons line up thusly, mathematical:
huge cloud line, pieced top, like reflected farm plots then
thin line of bright horizon and
then the ground.

INTERVIEW

You love your west. Your home.
I do.
Your rocks. Your landscape.
My mountains. My mountains.
So why do you want to work in Ohio?
I have a job in Ohio.
That simple?
Oh I would not say simple. Rock
is simple. Sand in the desert is. My job
in Ohio is not.
And how is Ohio different?
Ohio is not different.
When you say different do you mean
from itself or from other landscapes?
You said different.
I said different?
Look at the transcript.
So I did.
What I mean is that Ohio is the same as itself.
That seems clear.
In Ohio, I cannot tell field from field. I drive
past a field and cannot find
a mark to differentiate it
from other fields. I have no mountains
to orient my map,
I have no map in my head to begin with, only stops
on the route, as with a subway line.
You have no cardinal directions?
No scope. No freeway ramp
high enough to see it from.

High enough for landscape, you mean?
Not nearly landscape.
Could a ladder help?
Perhaps a ladder. Perhaps
I could use a very tall ladder. To take it all in.

LAY OF THE LAND

Listen: train, train.
It goes low, high
the high part lasts longer
low
low, high.
Cool window air
feet height
when I am on my bed.
On my radio
a dead guy sings.
Let's say it doesn't bother me.
Let's say there's no breeze
and I open the window.
Let's say no breeze I look out the window.
What does one do the land is flat.
No where for a breeze to start.
I am tired.
It takes more here to walk a dog.

*

A grocery store.
A gas station.
And Upground Reservoir,
built on the old quarry
where they removed the rock,
and Riverbend Park,
the prettiest spot in town but so flat
I can't tell which direction
the water is going.

Cooper Tires.
A cemetery, then the city edge,
line of trees
field field silo with an eagle
painted on its side
then a plain old silo then 12 more
exactly like it
another cemetery.
National Lime and Stone you can't see
from the freeway
Benton Ridge Sewage Lagoon
you also can't see
and the hole they dug
to build the overpass is
now filled with water, a campsite
right by the onramp
surrounded by trailers, and in the overpass pond
roiling screaming kids with inner tubes
then field field field quiet
line of trees
then a cemetery then
field field field field field.

*

And in the winter
the snow flattens things further
a two-dimensional version
of landscape, a map of itself,
flattens everything around it
flattens even the sky.

silo shade don't sit
directly in the heat
you want a halo don't you

don't get it that way go
read your letters stupid

your letters
↓

53

← here's where you go there's where you park your car ↘

POEM FOR THE PUTTING IN OF THE NEW CARPET

Findlay, Ohio

This day's a green one, breezed, wet with air.
I sit by the window, wonder
if I will become kind again
once the carpet is in.
I am far from home.
I am in a house I have bought I have
come far.

*

We put up a painting we have bought,
a painting with pieces of figures taken from Courbet
and spliced to other figures
one's part of a head that turns into
part of a hand that turns into—who knows?

*

I have painted the two desks green
the kitchen table wine rack
side tables a chair all green
the chairs around the table brown.
This is the stuff of our old families.
We have taken the stuff of our old families
and put a layer of green on.

*

How to hold
to have my house contain.
It keeps out the humidity keeps in the cool
and we will pay for it later for
all of it and our
secret togetherness, now housed,
is put down in a book
and calculated and summed
and the average part is
I have become cold.
Meantime the sky
is heavy without girth
like the wet air.
The sky is a blue roof and not.

*

When the sky is daytime blue
it is a curtain
drawn up over the stars.
At night, the curtain opens
to a flat map of the universe,
the near and far side by side,
one single surface.

*

They are putting the carpet in
right now as we speak
and up will go the green desks
and up papers and books
I will become kind or

I was never not kind
or I am what I always was.

*

Can I have your hand?
Can you put your hand on the top
of my head like a cover
and can you turn it on my hair?

*

Rooms become smaller
with new trim paint and nothing but scrapwood flooring.
It's an optical illusion—I was never blue.
Can't count on a house
and the calculations are already such that
I am green. Let's start again. Again.
Put it in, the carpet,
I need a bottom so as to catch me.

and here's the sun

can't you see darling
it's written right
all over your face

and here's
where
the house

OHIO

This day has a quietness
that sticks. The writing
makes a noise like sheets,
then a quietness.
Yesterday, a sky I could
live with. Day before, wind.
I pushed the side of my car
up against the great nothingness
of air, and it pushed back.
Yesterday the sky had height,
the clouds were measurable
and various. Dark and light.
The blue between the clouds was blue.

SHOWER WATER

stood in the shower today
let water drip off my lids
it wasn't crying
it was shower water
the top of my eyelids
if I moved back more water
if I moved forward less

a picture holds   the wide world

like looking out a window   at the sky

as if to shore up the sky

Port

BOAT TOUR

You will see to your left the new port
you will see to your right the old,
l'obelisque, to the left the clocktower,
only remaining piece of—
bombed by the Germans when they left,
now a great distribution center for fruit
all the way from Africa,
and the gulls on the roof scare
all at once, middle of the night,
all up in the air and yelling
their human yells, the fruit,
the stars, the war memorials in
three different languages,
bombed par Allemandes in 1944,
the waves are slight, very slight,
the water molecules, I am told,
stay in the same vertical trajectory
though they appear almost to be moving forward.

wave not wave

throw down   your sky

yellow to green   with girls on the mountain

up behind us

tornado mouthed

trip to the back porch

trip to the greenhouse

let's toast

FIELDGUIDE

is it a red one it is
desert paintbrush it is skyrocket
is it a pink a purple
shooting star is it a wild rose
primrose a morning glory
is it growing on top of a cactus
so prickly pear is it cold
out still glacier lily
can you blow the petals poppy, orange
desert dandelion blown white
it is a weed nonnative pull it
it is this or it is that one
I saw a purple bell upside down
the width of two fingers
I've never seen anything
like that way out here

FIELDGUIDE MARGINALIA

Flax

is not yellow as I thought
but purple blue, thin skinned
as poppies—Sue
has got a thick patch
posing for photographs
with whole mountains

Dandelions, late-stage

here there are bones—
Addie has a bone she found
growing as if from the ground—
and greens and honeybees and
the dandelions have overblown
but there's always another thing to be,
the puff of white seed only an early
stage of yellow

Valley lily

sweet bells, dress frilled
faced groundward like a little girl,
a picture book: a fairy in each
the bell is her dress part
wait till night only
the sweet

smell will
put you to sleep
take it for a nightcap, even

Radiotower violet

electric blue, blue electric purple
stacked as with signal

the whole meadow covered
all parts connected

Glacier lily

thin, but built for ice
meadow yellow
thin, thin stalked, then the field
turned to shooting stars,
not red like Sue said
but purple-pink, clumped
head first for the ground
petals back, a diver underwater
head first, a whole meadow wide
and the wind blows intermittent
grasses into brushed sea
this rapids, this blown grass

THREE POEMS CALLED "THE BASIL"

The basil

The basil wilted
clear to the side of the pot
and I gave it some water
and it's back now
I've quit my Ohio job I'm
better than ever

The basil

It is amazing the basil
how the water was sucked dry
its wilt and fall
how it took to the new water
and how back to normal

The basil

The basil is big
I trimmed it back to make it bigger
each break a double growth
each stalk tipping with
its own weight
I cannot write about my dead dog
he is dead
the basil I can write is big and alive

KEEPING TRACK

five birds on the wooden beam
black and shaking their luck
no six I missed one
it was there anyway

a whole page of possible directions
each little
blink of muscles and wings

on its own   arc
some even going forward

PROOF

Sue has put bird houses
in big colors
on top of posts
and if god, god has put a sky here
for a roof
and if red,
red has made itself a wagon for dirt
and if dirt, the tree has
planted itself in ingenuity
also the sage
as Sue has planted
a whole small garden plot

PHOTOGRAPH OF A FRIEND TAKEN AFTER
HE HAS DISAPPEARED

I take a photograph.
A telephone wire, a pole.
Nothing to see.
I write: I can picture you here.
I write: Walk out of the woods, Craig.
I write: Those woods, there. And now.
I write: Walk out of the woods I have taken
a photograph with an empty spot the empty spot is yours.
I write: Take it.
I write: I can almost picture you.

I AM WEARING A PINKISH SHIRT

and lo and behold you are wearing
a very pink shirt
life is short or so they say
there is a beautiful girl with a baby
her baby is not here
moths fly against the window uninjured
every single thing
with every single right thing

HYMN

A song. Praise be. And the whole congregation joined in. A song I sing to know where I am. Copied word for word from the old hymnal. #30 All Is Well. #92 For the Beauty of the Earth. A transcription. For the organ. For the choir. These lines correspond to the keys correspond to the bird sound. A printed version of the bird sound. An arrangement with an entirely other instrument. For use with the choir. For use with the congregation. A printed version of an audio version of a person singing. A record. A set of instructions. Notes rendered simultaneously, and in this order, and in this way.

THREE HOURS IN A ROCKING CHAIR OUTSIDE
THE BLUE-ROOFED BUNKHOUSE IN THE WIND

Four dogs and me all of us looking at the sage and how the wind blew at it calmly but determinedly. Violet was in front. Kili looked like a still photograph of a dog and Violet looked like a home film recording.

Addie tried to eat the deer leg so Kili snapped at her although Kili had not been herself trying to eat the deer leg and in fact did not want to eat the deer leg and in fact did not try to eat it even after she snapped Addie away. Addie stopped trying to eat the deer leg.

The wind stopped then started. Addie sat at my foot. Violet had rot holes in her teeth. Violet wanted only for me to scratch her head.

The wind blew at the grasses like a time-lapse recording of grass growing so that everything seemed sped up. Addie ran 100 feet away and Violet sat at my feet. Rita had been sitting this whole time in the grasses looking like a real dog in real time not a recorded or photographed dog. Addie found another bone.

Now I've caught you up.

The clouds are huge. They move quickly respective of clouds but slowly in visual comparison to the grasses and that is part of why the grasses seem so fast motion, so sped up. The mountains don't move at all but sometimes the clouds moving make the mountains look like they're also moving, an effect similar to what happens when a person lies on the ground in a snowstorm and looks up.

I am always on this porch wrapped in a blanket. There is always at least some wind. Picture this. The invisible wind. Its evidences. The wind can blow so hard that whole dogs blow over. I am always looking. I have tried to write it down. The ordinary world. When I did, and when I didn't, it was always still there.

A RECORD OF WATER YOU CAN'T SEE

The evening lights are a map lifting the city
above itself, its yellow face stretched,
the lit city visible from the moon but
missing key particulars, dark parts.

And the long lights from the port
bend like legs into the water
    left, left, right, kick,
and the water disappears in the dark, turns to
black blank space between moored boats, black hole,
the port's yellow lights
    dragged across the gape,
    long live sparklers, falling candlesticks,
which are not in the water at all,
are all that's left of its shape.

METAPHOR: DESCRIPTION, USES THEREOF, SIDE EFFECTS, INTERACTIONS, ETC.

A figure of speech. A shift. To mean in a new way. Mathematical. As in, equal sign. Or mystical. As in, I see myself there but I feel myself here. Words possessed. Or a consolation prize. As in, if I can't have --------- at least I can have ---------. A transference. From the Greek, to carry over. Crossing the bar. A name that means something quite other than what it says. Some substitutions must be made. If I can't have you, at least I can have the desert. If I can't have the desert, at least I can have a dog. Using the closest corresponding letters of an entirely different alphabet. A bird sound rendered in hyphenated lettering. A word with a picture on the other side. A flash card. A pointing back. To William Blake, as in, the --------- is a --------- because both are holy, holy, holy. A rose is a rose. If I can't have my dead dog, at least I can bite my own arm. Can grow the basil plant. Praise be. Holy arm. Holy basil plant. Holy blue roof. Holy photograph. Holy actual world. Equal sign equal sign equal sign. Holy equal sign. To point not to me but up and out.

MAP LEGEND

Rd: road
(Posts): lined w/posts
Wood: hand-hewn, Wire: hand-tied
The white dot: Violet the dog
Three black dots: the other three
Jerry: I love how you've planted the sage
Jerry: how random the pattern
(Ha): laughs
Sage: random pattern
Rain: rain on sage: rubbing a leaf in wet fingers
New configuration: see how the dogs have changed places
Car: see how the moving car changes the configuration of the dogs
Blue area: the bunkhouse roof
Blue area: sky, with missing parts
White: missing parts, clouds
White: still snow in the mountains
Rain: changes the configuration of the sage
Sprinklers: rotating, sourced from well water
Rain: turns the sprinklers up, but makes them seem less substantial
Rain: reconfigures

POSTCARD

A picture on the other side. A pointing back. A copy. With space for a small message. With space for a mailing address. No return. A pointing forward. A blank. An explanation. Roping calves at branding on Flathead Creek. Montana. Ohio. Livre d'Heures, mois de septembre. The color of the sea around Sifnos. The size of the mountain. The type of bird that was common. Looking ahead. A copy of the painting. For use with a stamp. A printed version. A copy of the castle. Of the page from—. A photograph of the dish with fish and tomatoes. Anchois de Collioure. Sans envelope. Out in the open. Word and picture as rivals. At odds. And I was there. And while I was there I spent a half an hour. A record. Thinking of you. And this is the size of the Blanchard River flood that year. Taken from above. And this is the size of the whole island. You can tell by the relative size of the small fishing boats. By the trunks of trees under water. By the people standing under the arch. Looking up. A scope. A miniature. And I was there. And I breathed the original air.

Directions

seems fairly clear, the way to the mountain

you don't need a map you just
look out where you're going

DIRECTIONS

Start here. Walk to here.
From here, go to here.
Stay here for a time.
Then, go here.
These things will be all around you.
Look around.
You'll like it here.
But you really must push on
until you get here.

can't catch
it can
just wait
just watch

a boat
cross
the whole
water

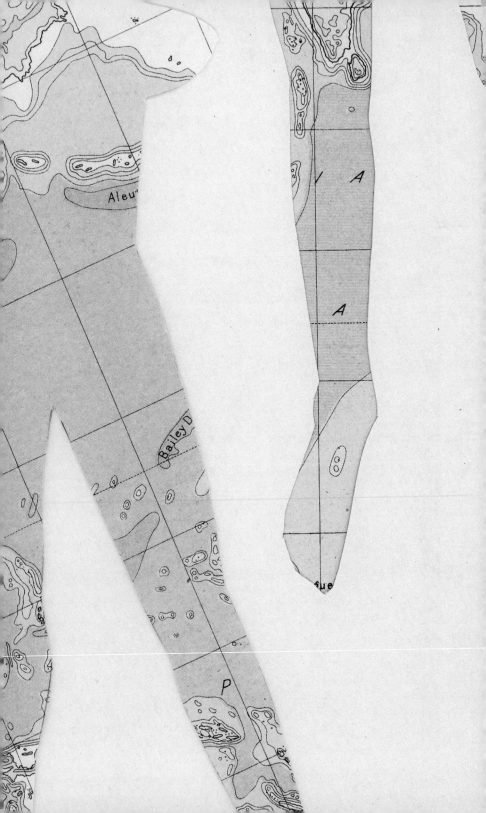

ACKNOWLEDGMENTS

Grateful acknowledgment to the editors of the following publications, in which poems from this book have appeared, sometimes under different names and in different forms: *The Best American Experimental Writing 2014* (Omnidawn), *Bombay Gin, Clade Song, Colorado Review, Drunken Boat, Flatmancrooked's Slim Volume of Contemporary Poetics, Forklift: Ohio, Free Verse, Interim, Kingfisher, The Offending Adam, Versal, Verse, Western Humanities Review, Witness,* and *Word for/Word.* Thank you to Cole Swensen, who selected "Map," "Fieldguide," and "Transcript" for the Academy of American Poets Larry Levis Poetry Prize for 2009. Many of these poems were made possible through the Snow-Neff Fellowship at the University of Utah; a pivotal travel grant from the Reza Ali Khazeni Memorial Scholarship for Graduate Study Abroad; a faculty development grant from Ohio Northern University; and faculty research grants and a Fisher Center Fellowship from Hobart and William Smith Colleges.

The support of a lot of good people made this book possible, so a lot of thanking is in order. First and foremost, thank you to Geoffrey Babbitt, my prime reader and friend and partner and coconspirator in life. And to my girls, the dearest best pieces of my whole world: Remi Blake, Calder Rae, Sobin Elizabeth, and Adeline Cloudpants too.

Thank you to Louise Glück, who spent hour after hour and visit after visit helping a perfect stranger rearrange her chronology until it finally made sense. I will never get over this gift you gave me, asking nothing in return. You are a wonder.

Thank you to everyone at Milkweed—to Daniel Slager for believing in this book in the first place, and to Jordan Bascom, Shannon Blackmer, Joanna Demkiewicz, Bailey Hutchinson, Joey McGarvey,

Kathryn Nuernberger, Lee Oglesby, and Mary Austin Speaker for their dedication, enthusiasm, acumen, and heart. Thank you to Heather Brown and Mind the Bird Media for teaching me to aim high and then giving me the tools, support, and encouragement to get there.

Thank you to my teachers and mentors, most especially Karen Brennan, Kate Coles, Craig Dworkin, Kathryn Stockton (from whom I borrowed "I see myself there but I feel myself here"), Susan Howe, Paisley Rekdal, and Jackie Osherow, and all the way back to Laurie Payne and Michael Rutter, who fired the first shots.

Thanks to my big beautiful blended family: David and Natalie Cowles, Delys and Phil Snyder, Leon and "Grandma Elizabeth" Cowles, Merwin and June Waite, Cristie and Steven, Rob and Erin, Steve and Brooke, Jack, Marissa and Brett, Liam and Ethan, Gary Babbitt, Cherie and Jim Clayton, Brooke and Chad, Laramie, Travis and Heidi, Kate and Alex, and all my beloved nieces and nephews and beyond.

Thank you to the dear friends who worked and reworked these poems in writing groups and who taught me how to be a writer and a teacher and a human being: Rebecca Lindenberg and Timothy O'Keefe (best witnesses/friends), Rachel Marston (who once saved me with a camp pad and open arms), David Weiss (a true friend and advocate), summer writing group-ers—Eryn Green (O Pan Fire! member), Nathan Hauke, Cami Nelson, Wendy Scofield, and Brenda Sieczkowski (for their support, inspiration, goading on, and martini sharing)—as well as Chris Abani, Hanna Andrews, Saedra Blow, Khalym Burke-Thomas, Harmony Button, Lara Candland, PJ Carlisle, Jeff Chapman, Jennifer Colville, Traci O Connor, Jackson Connor, Peter Covino, Kelly Craig, Shira Dentz, Danielle Duelen, Trista Emmer, Robert Glick, Susan Goslee, Natalie Green, Maddie Hanley, Derek Henderson (my twin), Matthew Ho, Brooke Johnson, Claudia Keelan, Stacy Kidd, Matt Kirkpatrick, Esther Lee, Julie Gonnering

Lein, Alice Letowt, Joel Long, Dawn Lonsinger, Christine Marshall, Susan McCarty, Joshua McKinney, Andrew Merecicky, Jennilyn Merten, Meghan Moore, Emily Motzkus, Deb Moeller, Jens Olavson, Julie Paegle, Michael Palmer, Christopher Patton, Jacob Paul Paul, Derek Pollard, David Ruhlman, Anne Royston, Mary Ruefle, Danny Schonning, Ely Shipley, Eleni Sikelianos, Nick Snow, Beth Spencer (and beautiful Bear Star Press generally), Claire Tranchino, Joshua Unikel, Nicole Walker, Lito Weiss, Mike White, and Khaty Xiong. Thanks also to Lucia Cardone, Carly Petroski, Sarah Taylor, Hanno Webster, Lindsay Webster, and all the other wonderful people who have provided childcare, giving me peace of mind and time to write.

Thank you to "Grandma Sue" Wicklund. You have changed the very way my eyes work.

Thanks to the friends and colleagues I've picked up along the way for their camaraderie and support, especially Robin Lewis (so glad we refound each other), Sue Gage (who keeps me sane), Tina Smaldone (who stops me from doing stupid things), Cáel Keegan, Melanie Conroy-Hamilton, Anna Creadick, Ingrid Keenan, Sarah Berry and Rod King, Taylor Brorby, James McCorkle, Kirin Makker, Kristine Johanson, and Ben Ristow. Thanks to my Fisher Center cohort—Cadence Whittier, Anthony Cerulli, Jess Hayes-Conroy, Brianne Gallagher, Keoka Grayson, Joe Mink, and Maggie Werner; to the HWS Center for Teaching and Learning, especially Susan Pliner; to the people who've supported the music part of all this, especially Rob Carson, Pablo Falbru, Brady Leo, and Mark Olivieri; and to my ONU friends, especially Druann Bauer, Doug Dowland, Eva McManus, and Rob Scott. Thank you all.

And finally, thank you to Donald Revell, "my teacher, now my friend," who taught me the shapes of the writing to begin with. Whatever you say, it turns out to be. How lucky I've been to get to be near you sometimes. Thank you over and over.

KATHRYN COWLES is the author of *Eleanor, Eleanor, not your real name*, winner of the Dorothy Brunsman Poetry Prize. Her poems and poem-photographs have been published in the *Best American Experimental Writing, Boston Review, Colorado Review, Diagram, Free Verse, Georgia Review, New American Writing, Verse,* the Academy of American Poets Poem-a-day, and elsewhere. Her poems were awarded the Academy of American Poets Larry Levis Prize, judged by Cole Swensen. She earned her doctorate from the University of Utah and is an associate professor of English at Hobart and William Smith Colleges in the Finger Lakes region of New York.

milkweed
editions

Founded as a nonprofit organization in 1980,
Milkweed Editions is an independent publisher. Our mission
is to identify, nurture and publish transformative literature,
and build an engaged community around it.

milkweed.org

Designed and typeset in Vendetta by Mary Austin Speaker

Vendetta was designed in 1999 by John Downer
for the Emigre type foundry. The design of Vendetta
was influenced by the design of types by Roman
punch cutters who traced their aesthetic lineage to Nicolas
Jenson's seminal 1470 text, *De Evangelica Praeparatione*,
a work of Christian apologetics written in the
4th century AD by the historian Eusebius.